FROM FRUSTRATED TO FLOURISHING

Accepting The Glory of Your Natural Hair

Ayana Charnette Martin

Ayana Charnette LLC

COLUMBUS, GA

Ayana Charnette Martin- Author

Ayana Charnette LLC- Publisher

Columbus, GA

Publisher's Note: This is a work of nonfiction.
Book Layout © 2017 BookDesignTemplates.com
Book Exterior and Interior Layout : Alexis M. Creative Agency LLC

From Frustrated to Flourishing; Accepting The Glory of Your Natural Hair
Ayana Charnette Martin
ISBN 979-8-218-58277-7

Dedication

Hey Curls Hey,

I dedicate this book to you! Your resilience is admirable! You've been knocked down, but you didn't stay there. By the grace of God you're reading the book Holy Spirit entrusted me to birth out. Even now your capacity to embrace your hair is expanding! Allow this book to encourage and remind you to always view yourself how Christ Jesus sees you! You have a safe place in between these pages to cry out, release the old, and walk in your new season.

" To the praise of the glory of his grace, wherein he hath made us accepted in the beloved."

—Ephesians 1:6 KJV

Contents

CHAPTER 1

Sis, I See You

There you are, staring into the mirror, your eyes shifting around your crowded bathroom, wondering how in the world you spent so much money on these natural hair care products, only to still look mediocre. Disappointed and confused, your hair looks nothing like the other women you see on YouTube and Instagram! You start to believe you're a lost cause. And so, the spiral of thoughts begins: "Should I go back to a relaxer or grab one of my trusted wigs and just make it through the day? Or maybe I can call someone to get me some braids, or even rock a silk press." Sigh. But that never lasts long. What should I do?

As your mind floods with these anxious thoughts, you become consumed by them. You have to think quickly because you need to get yourself and the kids ready to start the workweek. You're always busy, and you feel the silent pain of defeat and insecurity about your tightly coiled hair. Finally, you decide to gather your hair with a headband and call it a day.

I understand exactly where you are. Hi, my name is Ayana, your sister in Christ. My mission is to help you embrace the natural beauty of your hair within the pages of this book. It's time to come out of the spiral of anxiety, darkness, and defeat into His marvelous light! God calls you "Peculiar." Why do you think your hair is supposed to look like everyone else's? This guide will help you believe that you are fearfully and wonderfully made and that there is nothing wrong with your hair—or with you.

The Lord is so concerned about you that He didn't want me to start by teaching you about products or techniques. He wants to redirect you in love because He has heard your heart. As a hairstylist for over ten years, I thought I could write a book simply about caring for hair. But God knew you needed more: the capacity to fully receive His love. I knew He had called me to help women in ways that go beyond hair. If you're stuck on simply checking boxes, nothing will ever be good enough. You'll be on an endless cycle of searching and striving for validation from others. He wants you seated on a firm foundation, and that foundation is Christ Jesus! Are you ready? UmKay! Let's GO!

God is a man of war for His daughters (see Exodus 15:3)! He cares about how we care for ourselves and about the daily attacks we face from subliminal messages and cultural pressures telling us we're not enough. He wants you to cast your cares on Him because He cares for you, sis (see 1 Peter 5:7)! He is mindful of you and every single hair on your head. Your hair is part of your identity—an identity God created. Therefore, your hair is part of the "you" that He cares for, died to redeem, and wants to show His glory through!

This book may be centered on natural hair, but these divine principles can apply to every area of your life. How sweet is that? Yes, Sis, our Heavenly Father is all-inclusive like that! He wants you to know that He has made you accepted in the Beloved (see Ephesians 1:6). He accepts you because of who you are, and there's nothing you can do about it. There's nothing you can do! Nowhere you can go will ever separate you from His presence. Psalm 139:8

says, “If I ascend up into heaven, thou art there: if I make my bed in hell, behold, thou art there.” Sis, be content with what you have because God will never leave you nor forsake you (see Hebrews 13:5).

Put on your seatbelt! We’re about to embark on a life-enhancing transformation! I decree and declare over you that you will no longer view yourself as you once did, consumed by the world’s beauty standards. Even now, your thirst for acceptance and validation from others has dried up! Come forth, beautiful rose—fierce woman of God! You are anchored in Jesus Christ, our Lord and Savior. You no longer have to chase after trends because you are "HER"! Gone are the days of shrinking back and tiptoeing around others! Where you once walked on eggshells, now you have a way out! You have the power, through the Holy Spirit, to step on the enemy's head! Nothing will harm you—not even your feelings. I plead the blood of Christ Jesus over you! Take your rightful place as a daughter of the living and breathing

God! He calls you a "Royal Priesthood," not "nappy-headed." He calls you "Peculiar." So, Sis, claim your beautiful head of natural hair. Don't look at your length, texture, or color as less than. Instead, look to our Creator for His love, strategies, and divine inspiration to help you embrace the glory of your natural hair. In Jesus' name, Amen!

• CHAPTER 2 •

What Granny N Them Taught Us

Go back in time with me for a second. You just got home from school. 106 & Park is playing in the background. It's 2007, and tree braids have just come into style. You get to school, and one of the 6th graders asks you, "Why are you still wearing "little girl hairstyles?" For me, this is where the root of my issues with acceptance started. But let's go back even further, Sis.

Growing up, getting my hair done was painful and time-consuming. I hated it because my grandma was heavy-handed. The hot combs, pressing oil, the smell, the sizzling, the hits with a hair comb, the screaming, and the "Be still!" I was tired of her, and I know the feeling was mutual. "Honey, stop killing my head! Let me up so I can go outside and play!" Umkay?

The only thing about my hair in my younger years that worked in my favor was that I didn't keep up with the trends, which put me in a position to have healthy, long, and thick hair; besides, Grandma wasn't playing that.

I don't believe it was the fault of the previous generations of women who didn't know what to teach us or tell us about our hair. I believe many of them were doing the best they could and also fell to the pressure of trying to recreate what was socially acceptable. Most generations just repeat what they know. Now, I believe you and I have the divine opportunity to do it differently.

However, in school, the sneaky suggestions from our culture got to me, and I began to seek approval and acceptance from my peers. I had a neighbor, a high school girl, who took me under her wing. She styled my hair and gave me her hand-me-down clothes. I felt so beautiful with my flat twists, butterfly hair clips, and Apple Bottom jeans!

I don't know what some of your first hair stories are, Sis, but the truth is our culture has done a great job of pushing it's idea of beauty in our faces. We grew up watching 106 & Park, followed by Tresemmé® and Just for Me® commercials. Let's be real: we got the picture of what "beauty" and "good hair" were supposed to look like—long, thick, silky hair.

I grew up with my Just for Me relaxer, but nothing was silky about it. I thought that in order to achieve beauty, I had to look like the "It

Girl." My grandmother and my brother called me beautiful, but I only saw my shortcomings and flaws.

Then there was another problem that fueled my battle with comparison: not being raised by my biological parents. Without their affirmation and voice, I grew up without clarity about my life. This created a void of inadequacy and insecurity in my identity.

Who am I?

Am I wanted?

What is my purpose?

What is right for me?

Sis, have you ever been bombarded with these questions of who you are and where you truly belong? You're not alone, but we can't stay here in these thoughts! What I needed at this time—and what I believe you may need now is to conquer these thoughts—is a perception shift. Let's get to it!

CHAPTER 3

Perception Shift

PERCEPTION ACCORDING TO GOOGLE MEANS; "The ability to see, hear, or become aware of something through the senses. Another meaning is, "A way of regarding, understanding, or interpreting something; a mental impression." Synonyms for perception are: discernment, insight and wisdom.

What's your perception? What's your mentality toward your life and your hair? I believe the Lord wants us to evaluate ourselves in spirit and in truth. This can be a challenge if we are studying others more than ourselves. To know our identity is to know our creator. If we view ourselves behind distorted lenses, we are setting ourselves up to have a mindset of poverty, but God wants us to operate in His abundance. He is more than enough, therefore you are enough!

There are several principles that I am going to introduce to you over the next few chapters that I believe will help you transition from thinking beneath the word of God to coming into agreement with God's word!

I've listed the next three crucial chapters below to emphasize their importance.

Why? Sis, these chapters will guide you to a crossroad with understanding the need for a shift in your perception on life:

1. The Power of Forgiveness

2. Our Hair Our Glory

3. Bearing Spiritual Hair Fruit

In this season, I believe God wants to be open and honest with us. He wants us to have a genuine relationship with Him so that we can trust Him to purify us from stinking thinking. James 1: 21 says, "Wherefore lay apart all filthiness, and receive with meekness the engrafted word, which is able to save your souls." He wants us to grow.

CHAPTER 4

The Power of Forgiveness and Bearing Spiritual Fruit

AS THE LORD HELPS US UNLEARN AND LEARN HOW TO FILTER OUT WORLDLY AND FLESHY THOUGHTS, IT'S IMPORTANT TO UNDERSTAND THE POWER OF GRACE. Ephesians 4:32 reminds us: "And be kind one to another, tenderhearted, forgiving one another, even as God for Christ's sake hath forgiven you."

My journey to forgiving my family, my ex-husband, and several other people is what birthed and started this path of connecting our spirituality to our hair care and maintenance. I realized I haven't shared much about myself in this book because it's truly about you, but I sense that now is the time.

When I was going through my separation and eventual divorce, I was raising our two-year-old son, Moses, and had just given birth—or maybe I was still pregnant (that season was such a blur)—with our youngest son, Emmanuel. I was on a journey to achieve multidimensional hot pink hair. I wanted the best of both worlds: growth and rockstar hair color.

I had just begun my journey of understanding how to redeem time, length, volume, shape, and definition with my curls. It was 2020 during the pandemic, and it felt like God had literally shut down my entire world, both outside and inside my home. I felt like everything was falling apart.

Hair has always been my happy place. In fact, hair care, in general, kept me from sinking into depression. I am a Hairstylist who ministers behind the chair. Needless to say, I had a lot going on, and I was doing too much. It's important to pace yourself—or I should say, it is vital to give yourself grace when venturing out into unknown territory.

What does this mean? Well, let's just say that smack dab in the middle of a pandemic, separated in my marriage, and raising two sons alone, was not the best time to achieve hot pink hair and start a business. Yes, I said start my business! During this season, we all had to pivot, but I knew the Holy Spirit was calling me deeper into my purpose because I was in the wilderness. Umkay!

When I graduated from cosmetology school, I started out in a salon that specialized in silk presses and hair color. In 2020, I knew the Lord wanted me to understand natural hair in an entirely new dimension!

During this season, I was without a church home and homeless. My children and I moved back in with my grandma, and from there, we relocated to a shelter—literally and spiritually.

During the lockdown, I would see extremely defined curls on my Instagram timeline. I knew I could provide a service like this, but I felt defeated because I had little to no training and financial resources. Still, I stepped out on faith and started with what I could glean from videos. I began to replicate what others were doing with minimal resources and guidance.

This confirmed to me that I was hearing the Holy Spirit accurately. He was funding his vision, cultivating, and stretching me.

Give yourself grace, because what you are doing and where you are going, you've never done or been before. Take your time. Rest in God's timing, and lean on the Holy Spirit! He will bring all things back to your remembrance. He will guide you.

"Your word is a lamp to my feet and a light to my path" (Psalms 119:105 KJV). Proverbs 3:5-6 encourages us: "Trust in the Lord with all your heart and lean not on your own understanding."

Keep it real with God! Ask Him questions with an open mind and with expectation. Watch Him work, and—cue the song—"Hit 'em with that flex!" Then, watch God move with what little you know. Haha!

CHAPTER 5

Our Hair Our Glory

YOUR HAIR IS LIKE ANYTHING ELSE IN LIFE: GROWING, DYING, STRETCHING, AND CHANGING ALL THE TIME. If anything, it could be compared to plants. The Bible is full of plant metaphors because the people Jesus taught back in the day lived straight off the land.

John 12:24-26 (KJV) reminds us:

"Verily, verily, I say unto you, except a corn of wheat fall into the ground and die, it abideth alone: but if it die, it bringeth forth much fruit."

Your hair is meant to bring forth glory to this earth. It is part of how God adorns you with beauty. You may have heard the saying: "When a woman changes her hair, she is either about to change her life or already has!"

Our hair often reflects the changes life puts us through. When life is rough, our care for our hair often follows suit. This is why it's so important not to fall into the trap of comparison when it comes to our hair. You never know what another sister in Christ may be going through when it comes to her hair.

The next time you find yourself comparing your natural hair to someone else's, consider the bread aisle at the grocery store. You may be a Sara Lee kind of girl, while your inspiration photo might be a Nature's Own brand. Same aisle, same category, but cut from a different cloth.

The Holy Spirit gave me another analogy using fruit. He said, "Know the fruits of the Spirit. Seek Me on what season you're in, especially as it pertains to the fruit(s) of the Spirit being developed in you." He also wants you to begin seeing your hair as an actual edible fruit too.

According to Milady's Cosmetology Book, there are three different hair textures: fine, medium, and coarse. That's why, when clients, family, and friends ask me about their hair types and refer to letters and numbers like “4C” or “3B,” I respond with: “Girl, I don’t follow that chart!”

I then explain that the average head of hair often has a combination of fine, medium, and coarse textures across the scalp. Generally, medium textures dominate between fine and coarse hair. Understanding your hair texture is key.

Think about how we spend hours on the phone with someone we’re getting to know. That’s how we should spend time in God's Word. Why? Because we'll start learning His language, building a personal relationship with Him, gaining clarity and strength to grow in all areas—including hair care.

When you spend time with your Heavenly Father, He'll give you the grace to love and care for your curls! Through trial and error, you'll discover what works best for your hair by partnering with the Holy Spirit and consulting a Natural Hair Specialist.

Let's say that coarse hair is a grapefruit, fine hair is a banana, and an apple is medium hair. If your hair is more coarse like a grapefruit styling it like a fine banana would not give you high definition and longevity. If your hair texture is more apple medium you may have the most flexibility, but don't take it for granted. Even concrete becomes damaged by consistent water droplets over time.

Spend time with your hair. If you notice breakage, ask yourself: What's different now compared to my usual routine? Then, make the adjustments that best support your hair goals.

Now that we have more understanding on how to pay closer attention to physical textures and prevent mechanical damage, let's shift our focus to spiritual fruits. You need the fruits of the Spirit to flow in excellence, Sis!

Let's get into it!

• CHAPTER 6 •

Bearing Spiritual Hair Fruit

According to Galatians 5:22-23:

"But the fruit of the Spirit is love, joy, peace, forbearance, kindness, goodness, faithfulness, gentleness, and self-control. Against such things, there is no law."

Self-Control

Tell yourself No! or Not yet! or simply Nawl!—especially when you are in your wilderness season. God is about to do much with little! Sis, this is not the time to chase after Hot Pink Hair!

Gentleness

Your hair is like a plant or fabric. Handle it with care. Remember, you no longer have to conform to worldly standards of beauty.

Faithfulness

Show up for wash day. If you have to skip a day or even a week, be faithful by jumping back into the rhythm when you can. Persistence is key.

Goodness

Say goodbye to the "good hair vs. bad/nappy hair" narrative. The only bad or "nappy" hair is neglected and misunderstood hair. Your curls are worthy because God created them, and everything God creates is good!

Kindness

Be kind to your hair, especially while you're learning how to care for it. Progress takes time, so treat yourself and your hair with grace.

Patience

This journey is a marathon, not a sprint. Give yourself ample time to start and complete your hair care routine. Growth—both spiritual and physical—takes time.

Peace

Make peace with the inevitable frizz and shrinkage. These are natural parts of your hair's journey. We are striving for excellence, not perfection!

Joy

Laugh and smile when your hair doesn't turn out the way you envisioned. Throw on some cute earrings, add a pop of lip gloss or lipstick, and wear a big smile—especially during those so-called "little boy" or "ugly" stages. Whatever that means! Lol!

Love

The greatest of these is love. You are loved by God regardless of what you look like. It's okay, Sis—receive His love now and let it overflow in how you care for yourself.

CHAPTER 7

Reflection Questions

WELL MY SISTER, OUR JOURNEY TOGETHER is almost at a close but before you go, I want to give you some time to reflect, repent and journal through some of the things we talked about in this book. Here is a prayer to realign you with God:

Abba Father, Please forgive me for all unbelief, fear, and procrastination as it relates to our journey of me becoming not only an author, but your vessel in the earth in book form. Arrest my Sister reading this now! Under your power and anointing, allow your love to wash her! Wash away all shame from her past! Allow all of her pain to be a stepping stone to bring her closer to you! Thank you for the fresh revelation that you will share with her, revelations that only she and you know about! Sister, you will never be the same! Thank you Father for removing the scales from her eyes! Her perception is now yours! Thank you for creating in her a clean heart and renewing in her a right spirit! She can hear you more clearly now because of her obedience to continue reading! Abba cover her wounds up with your word! There will be no backlash as a result of what has taken place here! Only breakout, breakthrough, and breaking-forth! I seal her up in the blood of Jesus now! It's in your Son Jesus' mighty name I pray, Amen!

Embracing Natural Hair and Identity

1. How do you currently feel about your natural hair?

Write about the emotions, beliefs, or experiences that shape your relationship with your hair.

2. What messages have you internalized about beauty?

Reflect on how societal standards or family influences have affected your perception of beauty.

3. How do you see your hair as part of your identity?

Consider how your hair reflects your personality, culture, or spiritual beliefs.

Overcoming Societal Pressures

4. What societal beauty standards have you struggled with the most?

Reflect on how these pressures have influenced your choices and self-image.

5. What steps can you take to break free from these pressures?

Identify specific actions or affirmations that can help you embrace your natural beauty.

Faith and Self-Love

6. How does your faith shape the way you view yourself and your hair? Reflect on any scriptures, teachings, or spiritual practices that encourage self-acceptance.

7. What does self-love look like for you?

Write about ways you can show love and care for yourself, including your hair.

8. How can you see your natural hair as a reflection of God's design?

Consider how viewing your hair through a spiritual lens can transform your perspective.

Practical Hair Care

9. What are your biggest challenges in maintaining your natural hair?

Reflect on areas where you feel frustrated or need more guidance.

10. What does a healthy hair care routine look like for you?

Write about the steps, products, or habits you'd like to incorporate into your routine.

Personal Testimonies and Growth

11. What is your earliest memory of your natural hair?

Reflect on how this memory shaped your relationship with your hair.

12. How has your journey with natural hair evolved over the years?

Write about key moments, struggles, or victories in embracing your natural texture.

13. What advice would you give to your younger self about your hair?

Share wisdom or encouragement you wish you had earlier in life.

Affirmations and Commitments

14. What affirmations can you speak over yourself and your hair daily? List statements that build confidence and reinforce self-love.

15. How can you commit to honoring your hair's health and beauty moving forward?

Identify practical ways to care for your hair and maintain a positive mindset.

Building Confidence and Community

16. Who has inspired you in your natural hair journey?

Reflect on people, stories, or role models that have encouraged you to embrace your hair.

17. How can you inspire others to love their natural hair?

Consider how you can share your journey, advice, or encouragement with others.

ABOUT THE AUTHOR

Ayana Martin is a native of Phenix City, Alabama, and a graduate of Central High School (2012) and Columbus Technical College (2013). She is making strides in the beauty industry as a Master

Cosmetologist. With 10 years of experience, she has become an advocate for healthy hair and an expert in tight curls, hair color, and silk presses.

Her achievements include being honored at The Beauty Honors Awards as Favorite Silk Press Stylist in 2015 and Color Artist in 2020. Ayana is passionate about encouraging women to pursue Jesus while embracing the beauty of their natural curls.

Ayana is a servant leader and Evangelist at Kingdom of God Empowerment Center, with her spiritual parents, Apostle T.Q. and Prophet Dr. Charmia Martin. She is the Harvest Leader and also serves in content creation, Pur-Fya Worship Team, Children's Ministry and more.

Above all, Ayana treasures her role as the mother of her beloved sons, Moses and Emmanuel Turner, who inspire her to keep pressing forward through life's challenges.

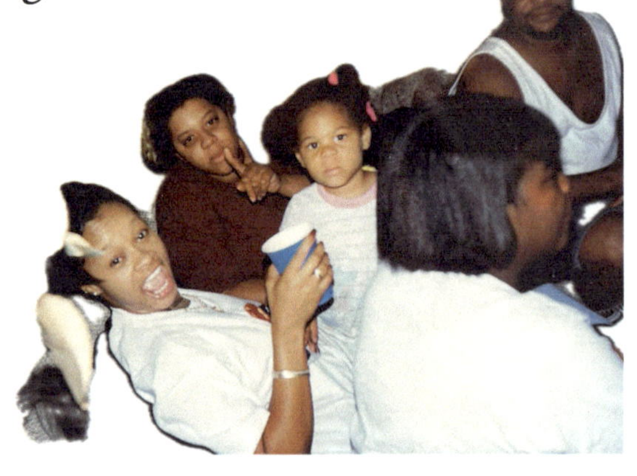

Works Cited

The Lord is a man of war: the Lord is his name. Exodus 15:3 KJV

Casting all your care upon him; for he careth for you. 1 Peter 5:7 KJV

To the praise of the glory of his grace, wherein he hath made us accepted in the beloved. Ephesians 1:6 KJV

If I ascend up into heaven, thou art there: if I make my bed in hell, behold, thou art there. Psalms 139:8 KJV

Let your conversation be without covetousness; and be content with such things as ye have: for he hath said, I will never leave thee, nor forsake thee. Hebrews 13:5 KJV

Wherefore lay apart all filthiness and superfluity of naughtiness, and receive with meekness the engrafted word, which is able to save your souls. James 1:21 KJV

"And be kind one to another, tender hearted, forgiving one another, even as God for Christ's sake hath forgiven you."

Ephesians 4:32 KJV

Therefore lay apart all filthiness, and Receive with meekness the engrafted word, which is able to save your souls.

James 1:21 KJV

And be ye kind one to another, tenderhearted, forgiving one another, even as God for Christ's sake hath forgiven you. Ephesians 4:32 KJV

Thy word is a lamp unto my feet, and a light unto my path. Psalms 119:105 KJV

Trust in the Lord with all thine heart; and lean not unto thine own understanding.In all thy ways acknowledge him, and he shall direct thy paths. Proverbs 3:5-6 KJV

Verily, verily I say unto you, unless a grain of wheat fall into the ground and die, it abideth alone; but if it die, it bringeth forth much fruit. John 12:24 KJV

But the fruit of the Spirit is love, joy, peace, longsuffering, gentleness, goodness, faith, meekness, temperance:

against such there is no law. Galatians 5:22-23 KJV

Made in the USA
Columbia, SC
18 April 2025